Wisdom the Strength of True Manhood.

A

DISCOURSE

DELIVERED AT SALEM, MASS., NOV. 13, 1866,

IN BEHALF OF THE

SOCIETY FOR THE PROMOTION OF COLLEGIATE AND THEOLOGICAL EDUCATION AT THE WEST.

BY

SAMUEL W. FISHER, D.D., LL.D.,
PASTOR OF WESTMINSTER CHURCH, UTICA, N.Y.

NEW YORK:
PRINTED BY JOHN F. TROW & CO.,
50 GREENE STREET.
1867.

"The thanks of the Board were tendered to the Rev. Dr. Fisher for his Sermon, delivered last evening, and a copy requested for publication."

Extract from the Minutes, Nov. 13, 1866.

J. Spaulding, Rec. Secretary.

DISCOURSE.

PROV. xxiv. 5: "*A wise man is strong; yea, a man of knowledge increases strength.*"

THERE are two things which it is well for us to observe in order to a full explication of this passage. There is a distinction between wisdom and mere knowledge;—not so much, perhaps, between the highest form of knowledge and wisdom, as between the latter and the more popular idea of the former; for knowledge is taken to be the acquaintance of the mind with the general truths of science, while wisdom is the practical insight into the relations of these truths, and the masterly tact which combines them in the best manner to effect good ends. And so we often see a man who has largely stored his memory with facts on a great variety of subjects, whose knowledge, therefore, may be styled great and various, who is at the same time, and in spite of these acquisitions, quite deficient in the power to arrange and combine what he knows, so as to effect important objects. On the other hand, we often see men, his inferiors in these general acquisitions, yet possessed of a remarkable capacity for understanding the relations of what they know to what they wish to effect, for concentrating the scattered rays of knowledge upon the purposes of life;

and for this reason they are in the practical, concrete work before them vastly his superiors. Now, the wise man of the text is the one who combines both these elements of power. "Through wisdom is an house builded; and by understanding it is established." Such a man is a true *builder;* his intelligence compasses alike the elementary facts and their combination in a work of true science. He can not only quarry the stone, but put them together in such order, with such compactness, solidity, fitness, and beauty, that they shall form a noble mansion adorned and fitted for his habitation. The common maxim, "*knowledge is power*," needs just this qualification. It is knowledge inwrought into the very thought and reason; knowledge assimilated, and so creative; knowledge that becomes part of the mind itself, as it originates and works to practical ends—that comes and goes as he bids it, and as a servitor waits to effect his purpose; it is such knowledge ripens into wisdom; such knowledge is the highest form of power.

The *second clause* involves an idea somewhat in advance of this, although substantively the same. "A man of knowledge increaseth strength;" that is, knowledge enhances the original, the native force. Men differ in original capacity as they do in feature, form, and physical vigor. But in all cases knowledge proportionally augments power, be it originally less or more. Some men are specially strong by nature; apt, ready, quick in apprehension, effective in execution. Such men will work their way, and make their mark in their generation, often with very few literary or scientific advantages. Burns will sing his lyrics; and they shall be full of the inspiration of a true poetic genius; they shall touch the chords of humanity's great heart, evolving responsive music, generations after the tongue that gave them utterance is silent in the grave. Hugh Miller, that still more complete and well-rounded representative Scotchman, shall hammer and chisel his way down into the profundities of the world's mysterious generation, and up to the heights of literary fame. Henry, the orator, "*nascitur non fit*," shall enchain his rapt hearers by the spontaneous outgushings of an eloquence strange and wonderful even to himself. But all such native strength, when it takes knowledge to itself, rises to a grander height, expands over a wider field.

On the other hand, there are those whose original natures have none of this imperial force; they never originate, they only reflect, and that but partially, the light of others. "Wisdom is too high for a fool." The heights of wisdom their wings are too feeble to scale; they are at home only in the simplest facts and commonplaces of life. Knowledge increases somewhat the little strength they have; but in this constitution of the realm of mind it is not practicable by any known process of mental discipline to impart to them a broad, far-reaching, comprehensive, or creative power. The mass of men crowd the space between these extremes of strength and feebleness, the archangels standing in the sun and the dwarfs who grovel on the earth. To them all knowledge comes as a means of lighting up the leaden eye, and quickening the torpid currents of the soul, vastly augmenting their powers and widening their sphere of influence. And thus we have before us the twofold proposition of the text: "A wise man is strong, yea, a man of knowledge increaseth strength."

Now, it seems to me wholly unnecessary, before such an audience, here in the heart of New England, where these thoughts are as familiar as the alphabet, to do more than briefly illustrate this truth. In point of fact, it is so clearly impressed upon the nature and form of man; it shines forth so distinctly from all his noblest works, as to be obvious to the dullest comprehension. The history and the organization of man at once reveal the fact that his strength consists not in his physical energy, but in his wisdom and knowledge. He comes into this world the weakest, the most dependent of living things. Another mind full of emotion, informed by reason, acting on principles of the truest wisdom, must minister to his wants, must plan and study and labor for him; must train him in learning, with a profound knowledge of his high capacities, until, after long years of such gentle and wise nurture, he rises to the stature of a man. Then, as he stands forth in the fullness of manly beauty, how utterly disproportioned is his frame to the mighty works he is to accomplish, yet how admirably is it constructed as the instrument through which the intellect is to reveal its ascendency, and knowledge is to win its triumphs over mere brute and natural forces! Erect in form, his eye surveys alike the heavens and the earth, as if, being made only a little lower than the angels, he was destined to ascend to the first when he has brought the second into subjection. Look at that hand, so small, so slender, so weak beside the paw of the lion or the bear, yet that hand built the pyramids, that hand reared the enormous temples of Baalbec, that hand hung high in midheaven the wondrous dome of St. Peter's. That hand, did I say? yea, rather the wisdom and knowledge of this mind within informing, wielding that hand, wrought all these demonstrations of strength. These, using this slight, this feeble thing; teaching it how to subsidize all the forces of nature, how to tame the winds and the waters, and harness them to do its work; built all the proud cities of the past and the present; whitened the ocean with canvas; subdued the wilderness; approximated continents; opened the pathways of commerce and over them poured the freightage of human life and the products of human skill with a velocity that almost distances the chariot of the sun. When the mathematician of Syracuse taught his countrymen, by a combination of lenses, to burn the ships of their enemies, he only demonstrated in a single instance the superior strength of wisdom; just that kind of superiority which belongs to man in distinction from the brutes; just that superiority which, since the origin of the race, other things being equal, has always given the victory to its possessors over mere physical energy. It is this which gave Alexander, Cæsar, Frederick, Napoleon their terrible supremacy in war; it is this which gave the feeble hand of our forefathers that irresistible momentum before which the hosts of savage warriors, as brave and hardy as themselves, faded and fell as the autumn-leaves fade and fall before the frosts of winter; and just so far as any nation embodies in itself this high element of power, will it advance and conquer, while nations vastly greater in numbers and brute force, but inferior in moral and intellectual culture, will decline, and, if they succeed not in the acquisition of this more vital power, must die.

The same thought finds an illustration in that higher region, when you ascend to those transcendent forces which give to a nation its substantive form, its organic life; to those laws, in obedience to which the mind and heart of a nation move for centuries with the steady and certain march of troops drilled to the command of a single will. You see that the strength lies not in material forces, but condensed and operative in the wisdom and knowledge of the few who in this rose superior to the multitude. Your Solon and Numa and Confucius, your Alfred and Mohammed and Charlemagne, your Madison and Hamilton—what separated them from the masses around them? What gave them an influence which throbs through generations and ages? what but this eagle insight, this intuition into causes and results beyond the ken of others; this tact and knowledge combined which impresses on their minds and works the stamp of wisdom?

There is, however, another region of thought—another field of action grander than these, where our proposition finds its fullest illustration. Man is allied to his Creator—made in his image; in communion with *Him* he truly lives; in the knowledge of *Him* he becomes truly wise. Even God himself is strong as he is wise. It is not omnipotence alone or chiefly that constitutes him sovereign; it is not this that attracts to him the hearts of angels, nor is it this mainly they adore when they compass his throne. It is that *wisdom*, fathomless, boundless, infinite, which has laid in eternity the immovable foundations of his absolute supremacy. This flames in the stars, and creates the harmony of their sublime march in the peopled vastness of the skies; this smiles in the flowers, glows in the sunshine, glitters in the snow-crystals, pours its wild music in the tempest, sleeps quietly where the everlasting granite ribs the world, comes forth arrayed in beauty when the soft breath of spring has wakened nature to her green and glad existence, throbs all through the forces of this material creation, but reveals itself to man most grandly and lovingly in the face of Jesus his Redeemer; this is the sublimest strength of God. And just as man rises to a knowledge of Him, as on his intellect and heart this likeness to his Heavenly Father is drawn most distinctly, just as a son he takes in true conceptions of this wisdom, and in his soul feels the beatings of responsive affections, does he, the creature of yesterday, wax strong even with the might of God. Then it is he runs and is not weary; he walks and is not faint; he ascends on eagle wings and receives into his intellect the opening grandeur and fullness of the infinite God.

And while the weak and the ignorant, when introduced into this sublime science, wax strong, yet even in this loftier department of knowledge there are subjective differences in power. The Church on earth has always had her cherubim, whose profounder knowledge and larger capacity for combining the truths of religion, so as to set them forth with special completeness and adaptedness to mould and elevate the world, have given them a just supremacy among the disciples, as wise and strong. She cannot, if she would, and she would not, if she could, strike from her glorious roll of confessors, martyrs, and holy men, her Moses and Samuel, her David, Isaiah, and Daniel, her Paul and John, her Origen and Chrysostom, her Jerome and Gregory, her Calvin and Pascal, her Wickliffe and Cranmer, her Baxter and Howe, her Wesley and Edwards—for they are those who stood the strongest among the strong, the wisest amidst the wise, emperors and kings in the realm of divine science. Think of the influence of such a man as Augustine, that converted gnostic and debauchee—think of him as standing on the borders of those ages of darkness which were rolling up forces from the bottomless pit to submerge the Church, and sending his light forward and across that sea of corruption, chaos, and night, until its rays enter the cell of the monk of Wittenberg, enter the intellect of that grandest figure in the Reformation, aiding to kindle there anew the pure light on the altar of the Church of Jesus. See Calvin, the Lawgiver of the Reformed Church, and Zwingle, its battle-axe, and Melancthon, its scholar, and Knox, its iconoclast, all sitting childlike at his feet, to catch the whispers of that voice which, over the dead centuries, spake to them the truth as it is in Jesus;—then read once again the text, "A wise man is strong, yea, a man of knowledge increases strength," and learn how vast, how profound, how full of perennial life, is that strength with which God sometimes clothes his chosen servants, as they ascend to the comprehension of some of His wisdom, and enter, heart and soul, into the glorious Temple of His Truth.

I have thus briefly illustrated the passage before us. Let us now consider it in its application to the object represented by this Society. That object is to aid in the endowment and support of Christian *Colleges* at the West. I propose to speak first of the work of a Christian College, and then the way will be open to bring home to your responsibilities the claims of such institutions in our Western, and I trust also our Southern, States.

What, then, is the design of the Christian College? What has it done to fulfil this design? The design of the College is just to assist men in obtaining precisely this wisdom which constitutes a strong man. It aims to impart such knowledge and such mental discipline as will greatly increase the native strength, and enable its students to exert a large, profound, and healthful influence upon society. I say it aims to increase the native, the original strength—not to *create* it. Colleges educate, they cannot create. Brains are the gift of God. Strong natural powers come directly from the creative hand of Infinite Wisdom. Holiness is open to all; the child and the hoary head, the giant statesman and the feeble plodder, who can do little else than carry a hod, are here on a level. But great mental powers are no more within a man's grasp than his bodily stature. Colleges may aid in developing a mind inherently feeble, but they cannot give it the highest strength. This is not their office. You may educate as much as you please, and yet you cannot make a William the Silent out of a James the Second; yet there will be Burkes and Websters, Edwards and Chalmers and Halls and Masons, towering up above the multitude of even educated men in the secure strength and clear sunlight of matchless wisdom. And to object to the College that it graduates some foolish, some impracticable men, is to object that it has not creative energy—that it has not robbed the All-wise of his sovereignty, and constituted itself the Plastic Power that impresses on all nature its original form and native force. All that the College aims to do is to improve and develop the original powers according to their susceptibility of improvement. It takes the student from the platform on which the common-school and the academy have placed him, and, just so far as he is capable of profiting by its discipline, endeavors to lift him to a still higher position. By working his mind through all the niceties of thought in language, and the invigorating processes of mathematics, and the great facts and theories of natural science, up to and along the line of those profounder principles which constitute the knowledge of his intellectual and moral nature, and so out into the broader field of the attributes and works of God; by teaching him how to abstract and analyze and penetrate through the outward appearance to the underlying principle, and then ascend to broad and massive generalizations, and thus incorporate knowledge into his soul by a true mental assimilation;—by all this varied process it seeks to make him strong in the noblest sense. A mind gifted with fine natural powers, availing itself of this discipline, grows unconsciously to a lofty stature; it becomes, on the one hand, a compound blow-pipe, in whose flame the diamond resolves itself into its original elements, all questions solvable by man lose their knotty hardness; and, on the other, a grand constructive force, under whose action chaotic facts wheel into system and order, and the world, man, providence, no longer a wild, rude, puzzling, confounding, disconnected, disarray of things material and immaterial, take each their places as parts of one harmonious thought, over which the wisdom of the Infinite sits enthroned in mysterious and unapproachable glory.

Nor is this all the College aims to effect. It recognizes the fact that a man who can write and speak, as well as think, is doubly strong; that such an one can make his powers most effective in moulding and elevating mankind; that he, coming into sympathy with humanity, can best infuse the light he has brought down from the throne into the eyes that are everywhere upturned to receive it; that he, seeing men groping in darkness, can most effectively seize the torch of truth, and cast its blaze full upon the errors and darkness of the world. And therefore the College puts a pen into the scholar's hand, and disciplines his stammering tongue, and awakens and invigorates his power of expression by the collisions of debate and the exercises of the class-room; and then sends him forth practised in the art of grappling with mind and bringing down to it all the researches of science and the acquisitions of practical labor.

Nor are we yet at the end of our College work. For here I speak only of a truly Christian College;

where God's word is made the highest authority; where this is sought to be inwrought into the reason, the conscience, and the heart; where all natural science is known to be its servitor, and itself the highest revelation of infinite wisdom; where week by week its teachings are brought to bear upon the whole man;—of such I say that it bids the ripe scholar go forth from its halls responsible to God for his influence; it bids him go forth as the friend of man, the deliverer of the oppressed, the comforter of the troubled, the guide of the blind, the support of the weak, the elevator of the corrupt, the enlightener of the ignorant; it bids him, no matter what walk of life he may choose, whether it be the pulpit, the bar, medicine, merchandise, the chair of an editor, or the profession of a teacher, remember that he is gifted of God with a special mission to commend the religion of Jesus to the hearts of men. It puts into his hand the Bible as a familiar book, that he has studied long and profoundly, and tells him, armed with this, to consecrate his powers to Him who gave them, and the Saviour who redeemed him; and putting his trust in One almighty to save, regardless of the babblings of infidelity, the taunts of the worldly wise, the ribaldry of the profane and the profligate, to go forward and do his best for the life that now is, and that grander life which must so soon open upon him.

Such is the design of a truly Christian College. It matters not that in all cases it reaches not full success. God only is perfect; God only accomplishes all His purposes. Man, imperfect in his nature, working with imperfect instruments, can attain only imperfect results. It is enough that the College seeks by all worthy means to effect this work in the mind and heart of all its students.

Now it may be said that all this may be accomplished by private tuition and discipline. Well, the College arrogates to itself no monopoly of powers to effect these objects. It is certain that a man of great natural force and rich gifts, may, with little of the machinery of the schools to aid, but at the cost of vast labor, work his way up to the heights of professional knowledge, and stand forth strong in wisdom. All honor to Franklin, to Summerfield, to Clay, who, conscious of high gifts, sought by steady labor to develope and use them for high purposes. Such men there are here and there in all the professions. Would that, instead of rising now and then like solitary palms in the wild dreariness of the desert, their name was legion, and their light a constellation amid the starry splendors of the firmament.

Yet, with all this admitted, it is affirmed, that just here the College asserts its supremacy as the finest means of helping forward to their just position this whole class of minds. For, think a moment, what a combination of circumstances and influences there must be to rouse, to bear up, to encourage those minds in this great work! Think of the obstacles they must surmount, the influences of physical pursuits and pecuniary success tending to draw them aside, and then wonder not that you can almost count their names on your fingers. The greatest, the best of these men are at one with us here. They are ever ready to acknowledge a consciousness of the lack of that breadth and accuracy of culture which the College gives, but which is rarely attained outside of it; while, as a general rule, it is evident all along the history of civilization, that the College, or some equivalent educational force, has brought forth minds thus gifted, and through its invigorating discipline, they have risen in multitudes to the heights of wisdom. This influence, going forth from these institutions, has roused the latent genius to conscious life; has begotten new aspirations in souls that would have slumbered on in the round of material pursuits; this nerved them to effort, led them on from the school to the academy, and the academy to the college, until they went forth strong in wisdom, effective in knowledge.

It has sometimes been asserted that the College is anti-democratic in its character and tendencies: an assertion more stupidly false and unhistoric never was made. It is false in history. The old universities of Europe, with scarcely an exception, were originally eleemosynary institutions established as public charities. Scholars entered them from all ranks of society. The peasant jostled the noble, and in the conflicts of mind most frequently won the victory. Barons and knights in the olden time never dreamed of monopolizing knowledge. The men who handled the battle-axe and whose grand argument was the sword, were not so foolish as to imagine that God had given them all the gifts of intellect and wisdom. It was from these universities emerged a new order of nobles—nobles knighted of heaven; gifted by God himself with high powers of intellect, there trained to overturn the old supremacy of a false aristocracy, the supremacy of brute force, and usher in the reign of intelligence, the sovereignty of knowledge. And it is mainly to these very universities, where the sons of poverty, possessed of rare original endowments, ascended the heights of learning in connection with a revived Christianity, that our modern society is indebted for its vast progress in a truly Christian civilization.

But the sentiment is just as false in fact now as it is in history. Who are they, who, with bright anticipations, are found in our colleges, with manly earnestness rising step by step through the stern discipline of study, asserting the native nobility of an intellect informed by knowledge? Four out of five are the sons of toil, nurtured where brawny hands hold the plow and swing the hammer. I see yonder, in one of the quiet intervales of New Hampshire, and not far from that lake which sleeps so beautifully among her hills, a father and his son riding together. That father was a man of the revolution, whose heroism had assisted to maintain our liberties, but on whose escutcheon there was emblazoned no heraldic signs of hereditary dignities. He had entered a section of land and built his log cabin on the frontiers of civilization, where, till then, the smoke curling upward from the bark hut of the Indian was the only sign of a human habitation. Time has passed on; the forests have disappeared before the axe of the sturdy woodman; Dartmouth College has been planted in part by the munificent charity of one across the waters, whose name it bears and honors, for the purpose of educating the sons of the forest, doing for us what it is the purpose of this Society to aid you in doing for our Western world. In the bosom of that son the desire to enjoy its advantages has grown strong. The father, too, impressed with the inestimable value of education, like all our Puritan ancestry, yearned to see that boy become an educated man. Long has he pondered how, with his slender means, to secure that great object. At length, though it cost him a sacrifice only those placed in his circumstances can fully appreciate, his desire ripens into a fixed purpose. On that wintry morning, as he rides slowly along, he informs his son that to college he may go. The manly boy, too full of emotion to speak his thankfulness, leans his head on his father's shoulder and bursts into tears. There is a picture of struggling poverty in its intense and passionate longings for high intelligence, worthy of the pencil of the most gifted artist. You all know the result of that lofty purpose; what name stands forth preëminent among the sons of Dartmouth; what name within the last half century has been blazoned in letters of living light all over the pages of his country's history. It was the College that trained the stalwart intellect of Webster; it is the College that, at this time, is busy in giving the power of knowledge to the minds of hundreds of the sons of just such fathers.

From these seats of learning the blood of a new intellectual life is poured into the veins of society. Never can a nation become effete and old where Christian Colleges are sending forth, into its positions of power and intelligence, minds fresh from all the departments of social life, with their original and special associations, refined and energized by a noble Christian intelligence.

Right or wrong, the influence of the College has always been profound and far-reaching. In some cases and for a season they may have been the fortresses within which error has entrenched itself, and then their power for evil has been terrible. But in the main, the great republic of letters they have constituted has been a power for good, elevating society, beating down the tyranny of hereditary station, and sending its light far and wide. Out of the universities have gone forth the great leaders in Church and State; the men who have initiated healthful reforms, originated free, ecclesiastical organizations, systemized and given form to law, framed constitutions to check and fetter irresponsible power, worked with an enlightened zeal in all the professions, as statesmen, as lawyers, as physicians, as ministers of the gospel, as teachers, as editors, and given to society the ideas and the spirit which are now spreading themselves as the elements of a nobler civilization than the world has ever seen.

Such men, to a large extent, led forth the colonies to this new world. The Robinsons, the Davenports, the Mathers, the Penns, the Ogilthorpes, gained their power in the universities. All along through the Revolution and the formation of our Constitution, it was the men of a thorough education that bore the most effective part. Washington and Franklin were the exceptions to a rule. The men who drafted declarations, who negotiated treaties, who framed constitutions, who administered governments, who interpreted the law, who gave to our institutions their peculiar vitality, compactness, and form, were mainly educated by a generous literary discipline, for which most of them were indebted to those infant institutions which, with benevolent foresight, our fathers had planted. Macaulay's remark of the great men of Britain is substantially true of this country. "Take," says he, "the Cambridge calendar, the Oxford calendar for two hundred years; look at the church, the parliament, the bar; and it has always been the case that the men who were first in the competition of the schools were first in the competition of life." Take the calendars of the Colleges of this country since its settlement, and the great mass of those who have shone as the brightest lights in each generation, and who in all departments of mind have achieved the noblest triumphs, whose works live either in the form of books, or statutes, or institutions, or men informed by their spirit, will be found there recorded.

Especially when you come to the Church, to train whose sons for the ministry Colleges have been largely endowed, is this remark true. From a fourth to a third of their graduates have entered the ministry. Here they have wrought patiently, quietly, earnestly, and with an effectiveness it is almost impossible to over-estimate, to instruct and elevate society, through the illustration and application of those Divine truths which, like the sun, are most mighty to bless the world. In our own land, or far away in Turkey, in Hindoostan, in China, in the islands of the sea, they have scattered the seed which is now yielding so rich a harvest.

Thus doth the College send down its influence through society. Its elevating virtue penetrates to the remotest limbs of the body politic. The minds it has trained transfuse the thoughts that quicken and the science that stimulates and guides into multitudes that know not their source. They enter an atmosphere of thought, which men breathe, and feel its quickening power without realizing whence it comes. Its noblest triumphs are not the grand displays of its orators, the writings of its philosophers, or the arguments of its statesmen, but that insensible influence which, proceeding from many sources, imparts a vital energy to all the noblest functions of society.

Could the educated minds that have informed the world be marshaled before us in one grand army, what an imposing demonstration, rising to the sublime, would that scene present! Moses, reared in the temple of Isis, the great college of the Egyptians, should head the procession of the ancient hierophants of science; Socrates, Plato, and Aristotle, should lead forth the corps of philosophers, historians, poets, statesmen, and orators, educated to the highest point of mental power in the schools of Greece; Cicero and Tacitus should gather around them the cultivated mind of Rome; Paul, reared at the feet of Gamaliel, should marshal the hosts of Christian scholars, trained in the seminaries of the early Church; Jerome, with Wickliffe and Tyndale, should march before the company of those magnificent scholars who have made the Bible a household book, bearing before them God's Word translated into the vernacular of one hundred and seventy nations, all blazing with the light that, through its various languages, shines upon six hundred millions of our race; Augustine and Calvin, the grand masters in the realms of theologic science, should assemble the profound thinkers who have given form and symmetry to systematic theology; Luther and Wesley should bear a burning torch before the Reformers in Church and State; Bacon and Descartes, with calm, philosophic mien, should lead the hosts of philosophers; Grotius and Montesquieu and Mansfield, the bench and the bar; Paracelsus and Harvey and Cullen, the physicians; Chrysostom and Whitfield and Chalmers, the orators of the Church; Mirabeau and Burke, the orators of the State; Spencer and Milton and Johnson, the poets and critics and writers in the field of literature; and thus, under these great leaders, the vast army who, in all the departments of thought and influence have wrought for man, should pass in review before us. The historians, the editors, the teachers, the men whose thinking has been for man, and has told deeply on his progress and destiny, would all combine to form that matchless demonstration of the elevation, the glory, and the influence of educated mind. These, and such as these, the College now aims to mould and multiply through the length and breadth of our expanding land. The Edwardses, the Dwights, the Witherspoons, the Davises, who are to train the thinkers for our future, are to come forth from the College; the Hamiltons, the Jeffersons, the Storys, the Kents, the Clintons, the Websters, are there to ripen their genius for their future work. The men who are to write our best books and rule in that mighty fourth estate, the weekly and daily press, and minister as our physicians, and teach in our academies, are there to gain their chief discipline. The ministers of Jesus, whose words uttered from thousands of pulpits, spoken in love and hope by ten thousand firesides, sounding afar amidst the darkness and silence of Paganism, until prophecy is fulfilled and Jesus ascends His throne on earth, are there to obtain in large part their preparation for their sublime work.

Such is the character, the purpose, and influence of the College. Under right influences its whole design is to develop the wisdom which makes the man strong, and impart that knowledge which increaseth strength.

This discussion of the real work of the Christian College is the strongest appeal to the best feelings of all right-minded men to plant and sustain such institutions wherever they are needed. No true patriot can be indifferent to their claims when he fairly apprehends their character and aims. Two hundred years ago it was remarked by one of the great patriots of our country, "The nations that have shaken off barbarity have not more differed in the languages than they have agreed in this one principle, that schools for the instruction of young men in all liberal sciences are necessary to produce and preserve that learning which softens the manners and saves from rudeness." Colleges, representing the higher grade of mental cultivation, and connecting themselves with all the science which is diffused through the State, have always attracted the deepest interest of our most enlarged and patriotic minds. You can scarcely name a person in the history of our country distinguished for comprehensive views and regard for the interests of the State, who has not evinced his appreciation of the College as a power vital to our elevation. As founders of such institutions, as benefactors, as supervisors, as generous and ardent friends, their names have acquired an additional lustre; they have connected themselves with powers that would live and work for the elevation of the State and the preservation of our liberties long after their bodies had mingled with the dust. They felt that virtue and intelligence were the only forces competent to secure a free, a prosperous, and a highly civilized society. Without these in a republic, constitutions, laws, popular suffrage, were only ropes of sand; with these our nation would survive all the assaults of its enemies from without, and the more deadly assaults of the ignorant, the corrupt, and the traitorous within. Who is there that cares for his country, who loves her liberty and glories in her progress, and hopes to see her the foremost representative in the congress of nations, of all that is most noble and beneficent, that can say, These institutions are nothing to me; I recognize no claim of theirs upon my influence, my property, my efforts?

But if patriotism should feel and act thus, what shall we say of the obligations of the Church? If Jesus has led his people to institute these powers of light, where is the Christian who can be indifferent to them, who will not recognize them in his prayers, and will do nothing to secure them as forces vital to the advancement of true religion? The relation they sustain to the Church and the progress of Christian truth, is of incalculable importance. Cotton Mather says, "A college was the best thing that ever New England thought upon." And the testimony of the early colonists was to the same effect. "After God had carried us safe to New England, and we had builded our houses, provided necessaries for our livelihood, reared convenient places for God's worship, and settled the civil government, one of the next things we longed for and looked after was to advance learning and perpetuate it to posterity; dreading to leave an illiterate ministry to the churches, when the present ministry shall be in the dust." There outspoke the heart; there shone forth the Christian foresight of those heroic men who laid broad and deep the foundations of the Church and State! "They dreaded to leave an illiterate ministry to the churches, when their present ministers were in the dust." They looked to the future; they labored for posterity, and we have entered into their labors, and are reaping the harvest. This is the spirit which has made New England, in her religious character, her civil and literary institutions, the glory of our nation and the wonder of the world; this has given to her sons that high intelligence, that power of personal impression, that persistent and clear-sighted enterprise, which all over this land is to-day the finest demonstration of the wisdom of a Puritan ancestry. This high appreciation of learning, beginning with the common-school and culminating in the university, has moulded the character and is yet to fix the destiny of millions. This taught her bayonets to think, and compacted her troops into a solid phalanx by the power of principles clearly seen and deeply felt. This, in connection with her position, developed her inventive genius, and has made her valleys vocal with the hum of innumerable factories. This has made her foremost in enterprises to spread religion and intelligence and liberty over the continent and the world. For a learned university, vitalized by the religion of Jesus, is a power the strongest in the world for the upbuilding of all sorts of institutions of learning and the diffusion of the thoughts that quicken and expand the souls of men. A learned Christian ministry and schools of science are ever related to each other as reciprocal causes and effects; powers acting and reacting on each other, and on the whole mass of society.

Now, that which they did for us we must do for those who are to come after us. With our advancing intelligence and our greater facilities, we must breathe their spirit and follow out their line of action; we must do what they did for the Church—the Church as it is yet to expand over this fair land and through the world. The College and the Church are bound to each other. The College must be consecrated by the Church. Her prayers, her sympathies, her watchful guardianship must encompass and sustain it; then the College will educate her ministry, and send forth trained intellects in sympathy with her spirit, and thus, and thus only, will the Church feel through all her functions the strength and influence of a consecrated learning.

I have said that the College must be consecrated by the Church. Christianity is a vital element in the progress and perpetuity of all true science. That science which begins and ends with man, which either has not God as its point of departure or its end, is shallow, effete, and powerless to elevate the soul. Separation from God is scientific suicide. Degenerate itself, it allies itself with human degeneracy, and hastens it, enervating the forces that would counteract it, turning the thinkers of the world into Pantheistic dreamers, and the people into dumb, driven cattle, for whom the brothel and the grog-shop are found just as excellent in educating them for eternity as the Church of the living God. Religion alone will save science from putrefaction, for it alone supplies the vital element which makes it a power to quicken and exalt the soul. And this power must be predominant, fully recognized, actively at work in these higher institutions, vivifying the mind, controlling the hearts, exalting the aims, purifying the utterances, consecrating the whole influence of the teachers in them to Christ and his Church.

The question here arises,—and it is a question which the logic of facts and the necessities of the case is forcing the Church to answer,—how can this religious influence be thus made predominant and secure in these higher institutions? No one will contend that the mere general influence of the pulpit at home is sufficient for this purpose; for our youth are gathered together away from home, under a peculiar discipline, to be moulded and impressed by men of learning and ability. By a law most powerful in its operations, the teacher standing for the time in the place of the parent, when the mind is just opening to thought, and is passing through the most critical period of its intellectual as well as religious life, may ennoble or degrade, may guide it into truth or pervert into error, may fortify its faith or strip it of its support, may lead it to Jesus, or send it wandering off into the night and frost of unbelief. The Church has no security in this line of action. In point of fact there are but two methods open to us. The first is, to commit the whole matter of education to the State. Now, if the State were in all respects truly Christian; if our legislators and executive officers were Christian men, of broad and comprehensive views, who appreciated the importance of a truly Christian education, and were resolved to secure it, we might safely follow this course for a time; although, looking at the future, and taking warning from the past, I should be doubtful of its expediency. But the State is only in a homœopathic sense Christian. It is composed of all sorts of people, separated by all varieties of belief and unbelief; and every one of them has just as good a right to have a voice in this matter as his neighbor. Organize your College on this basis, and every sect will demand that it shall be represented there; the Romanist must have his representative, and the Universalist his, and the Pantheist his, until your seat of learning becomes the arena of warring elements, and the result will be that Religion is utterly eliminated as an educational element.

Besides, we claim to be a free people, and in this sense we certainly are free; there are no legal hindrances, no State inhibitions, that shall prevent any denomination, or any portion of the people, or any one man, from establishing such institutions of learning as he or they may choose, provided the bare limits of absolute immorality be not overpassed; and the result will continue to be here as it has been, that Colleges will rise in the interests of different sects and of no sect; they will teach error or truth according to the influences that control them; they will blight or they will bless society. No man can legally prevent them. We must work in religious education according to the free developments that characterize the genius of our nation. The Church is to fight this battle on the basis of entire freedom, trusting not in the State but in God and his Word for the victory. And if she cannot succeed on this platform, she ought to fail; and this brings me to the only method really open to us for securing in these institutions of learning a thorough Christian education—an education in which religion shall form a vital and controlling element. The College should have one or more evangelical denominations of Christians standing back of it, pledged to sustain it, exercising a controlling influence over it, using it as an instrument the most powerful to advance religion and train her youth to fight the battles of the Lord. The Church is responsible to God for the Christian education of her sons. It is not for her to commit the training of the lambs of her flock to wolves, whether they wear sheep's clothing or their natural costume. It is for her to educate not only her own children in Christian principle, but, so far as her influence and resources can effect it, the youth of the nation. She is to aim at grand results. Nothing less than universal dominion for Jesus should measure her ambition and her efforts. This Society is the child of just such views. It sprang from the necessities of the Church in giving practical effect to this great idea. The question of denominations has ever been subordinate. Its first point of inquiry has been, whether the institution that asks its aid is under such religious control that true Christianity will be taught there; whether its teachers and its teachings combine to advance the cause of Christ? And when assurance of this has been given, then its strong arm has been extended to assist its feebleness and make it strong to fight the battles of Immanuel. It chose the West for its field of labor, because it was in its infancy, its immaturity, its feebleness; because there our sons and daughters were to dwell; there was to be the seat of empire; there, if anywhere, the vision revealed to our fathers of a Republic consecrated to Jesus was to be realized, and because there the assistance given early would tell with greater effect on the future progress of religion. The West was to us what the Colonies were to the fatherland. In the early feebleness of our institutions of learning, we stretched our hands across the water for help; and there is not one of our older institutions that did not receive it. But we were homogeneous; our ministry and people were animated by the same spirit, they appreciated the importance of the College, and they wrought together to build it up. But the West is heterogeneous, representing in itself the opinions, the prejudices, the excellencies, and the vices of all parts of this nation; and thus the difficulties in the way of consolidating and uniting the people in support of institutions vital to their future progress, was vastly increased. It was young, however; it could be trained; and they who early set themselves to the work of moulding the public thought and feeling, would be most successful. When a stream first begins to flow over a virgin soil, it wanders here and there without aim, for it has not found a channel in which to concentrate its powers. If now you strike a furrow, or dig a channel for it, as it follows it increases, it deepens, it broadens—you have fixed it for all time. But if you neglect it, it will mark out its own channels, and as it increases, rushes impetuously, carrying ruin to the fairest prospect. Then you may dyke, and dam, and work to regain your lost opportunity, which yet you will never fully regain: what might have cost a few thousands, now will cost millions, and labor infinite. The population of the West is such a stream. Wherever you have dug a channel for its thought, it has concentrated itself and become a tremendous power for good; where error and infidelity have anticipated you, or it has been neglected by Christian men, there, with equal force, it moves in divergent and evil channels away from the Church of Jesus. I need not speak of the West as the grandest field of labor for Christian men on this or any other continent; she speaks for herself. She is not to-day what she was yesterday; nor will she be to-morrow what she is to-day. The centre of power in this nation has reached already the Miamis; to-morrow it will be on the monarch river of the world. You began your work in what you thought was the West. You have reared your memorials there; institutions you aided in their feebleness, are mighty elements of power. To-day, across the plains of Kansas, across the Sierra Nevada, across the new-found Ophir and Golconda, where the Columbia pours its clear waters into the Pacific, and the Golden Gate opens its portals to the kingdom of the Orient, voices reach you pleading for assistance, to plant there those seminaries of learning that shall train a ministry for Jesus—a ministry that, passing westward, shall reach the East, and on the shores of Japan and amid the dense darkness of China, shall yet rear the standard of Jesus, and shed forth the light of a purer Christianity upon her myriad myriads of idolaters.

This is the age of enterprise, of vast, of gigantic enterprises, involving not thousands but millions; enterprises that, half a century ago, would have seemed as fabulous in prophecy as the tales of the Arabian Nights are in fact; enterprises individual, corporate, national, international, distancing the wildest dreams of the past, and equalled only by the magnificent imagery of the Revelation of the seer of Patmos. The nation and the world moves forward with strides majestic and sublime, such as the angel of the Apocalypse, who stood with one foot on the land and one on the sea, might fully symbolize. All the forces that create power and mould nations—commercial, mechanical, agricultural, literary, social, political—are working with an effectiveness truly grand. In this uprising and mighty march of humanity, all forms of good and evil are mingling and struggling for the leadership. Who shall be king, Jesus or Satan? What shall be the spirit that is to control and guide this immense force of mind in these its world-wide movements, Christianity or devilism? These are questions for the

Church of Jesus to answer—to answer only by deeds and not words—by deeds as grand, as vast, as comprehensive, as the forces she is to meet and master. No half-way, timid, feeble efforts on her part now will meet the measure of her responsibilities. With her vast resources, with all the experience of the past to guide her, with so sublime an object appealing to her faith and Christian heart, it is for her to rival and outdo the world in its gigantic projects. Error and infidelity are in the field, planting seminaries and colleges for secular education, where Christ is to be discrowned and Nature exalted to the throne. Millions at this hour are poured forth, in the attempt to subsidize the science of the world in the interests of error. If ever these influences prevail in our high places of learning, and the Cross becomes there the symbol of fanaticism and folly—if ever infidelity shall infuse its poison into the minds of our young men of genius and talent as they leave these institutions in all the strength of culture and knowledge—then will our land soon feel the sad eclipse of faith in its chill, dark reality; then will our pulpits be filled with men who, under the guise of religion, will preach the philosophy of Hume and Strauss and the magnates of satanic literature; our press will be ruled by a taunting, scoffing crew of the disciples of some modern Voltaire; our bar will abet injustice and crime; our physicians will deal with man as material and mortal like the brutes; our schools and academies will drive out the Bible and in turn die out, or become the hotbeds of corruption; then will come the triumph of the arch-enemy; licentiousness and intemperance, fraud, ambition, and violence will hold high carnival, and upon the nation will settle a darkness more fearful than that of Egypt in the night of her woe.

But if the Church, appreciating her position and responsibilities, shall put forth her power along the various lines open to her sanctified enterprise; if she shall not only plant churches but schools and colleges to train a ministry for them prepared to do Christ's work among the people, then no vision of the prophet, however bright and grand, will surpass the glorious future of our country. For these Christian Colleges, enthroning the Bible as the only true light of the immortal soul, shall rise and flourish in every State of our vast Union, and mingle their radiance till it covers with its glory of science the whole field of educated mind. Our gifted sons, breathing its pure atmosphere, shall become centres of spiritual power and light; our pulpits will be filled with men strong in wisdom and mighty in the Scriptures; our lawyers, trained under such influences, will plead at the bar, and our statesmen will legislate in our Senate-houses, as men who know that all law and all justice have their original in the bosom of God and their noblest illustrations in his blessed revelation; our physicians shall not only minister to the body, but to the soul they shall also minister the consolations of the Great Physician; our academies and schools shall feel the quickening influence descending and resting upon them. We shall rise to still higher regions of knowledge; we shall grow strong in the faith of Jesus. Our country shall grow wiser and purer, because it shall come to feel, through all its organs of influence and social life, the vital force of divine truth. We shall become, in all things true and manly, the glory of nations; and from us shall go forth the light of civil and religious liberty at one with the light of revelation. We shall carry back the law to the land where first the temple of God was reared; we shall bear the torch of truth into the darkness that enshrouds Hindoostan and China; the sons of Ethiopia in this land, led out of the house of bondage by an arm mightier than that of man, educated for God, shall consecrate many of their most gifted and eloquent ones to the evangelization of their fatherland; we shall give a noble civilization to the myriads of the great hemisphere on which we dwell; millions in every land shall hear the voice of our Christian teachers, and feel the force of our example; and then, then at length we shall join our triumphant voices in that grand chorus, which, from mountain-top and valley, from island and ocean, shall swell up to *Him* who bought us with His blood, and opened the portals of heaven to our sinful and suffering world. And now unto the King eternal, immortal, invisible; the only wise God; and unto the Lamb who sitteth in the midst of the throne, be honor and glory, dominion and power, for ever and ever. Amen.

www.ingramcontent.com/pod-product-compliance
Lightning Source LLC
LaVergne TN
LVHW020742120826
845150LV00010B/2346

* 9 7 8 1 4 1 8 1 9 4 5 6 7 *